Wis
About Relationships

Spiritual Reflections & Recovery Journal

Joseph C. Buccilli, Ph.D.

Recovery Communications, Inc.
P.O. Box 19910 • Baltimore, Maryland 21211 • (410) 243-8558

The information presented herein is
not intended to be considered
counseling or other professional
advice by the publisher, author, or
contributors.

Book design by Belle Vista Graphics

Printed in the United States of America

Library of Congress Catalog Card Number:
97-067363

International Standard Book Number:
0-9615995-4-5

Table of Contents

Present Function Despite Past Dysfunctions

The How-To of Making Boundaries

How to Accept and Like Reality in Relationships

Special Sections

Dedication

In celebration of my commitment to
my lovely wife,
Joann,
who continues to give me much more
than I have ever given her
and who persistently nourishes
the spiritual wellspring in my life.

I also dedicate this book to
all of the many "decent folks" who
have shared a part of their lives with me
over the past 47 years.

Acknowledgements

Special thanks to: Pat Alt, Sue Brown,
Cheryl Fortman, Steve Johnson, and John Pearson.

Introduction

Over my years of counseling and facilitating workshops, I have come to see that the greatest difficulties we human beings encounter center around relationships.

That rare man or woman who grew up in an unconditionally loving and supportive family may not find relationships difficult. But for the rest of us who may have grown up in a dysfunctional family, suffered early physical or mental abuse, or are recovering from addictions, relationships can be as bewildering as anything we know.

This book, intended as a relationship companion for every such person, is grounded in respect for the sacred spirit inside every human being, respect for the Creator Spirit above all.

My hope is that *Wise Stuff* will be one of those books you come back to again and again, as life presents you with ever-new relationship possibilities. After you have lived with its content, I would like to hear from you how it has been a help in your journey.

— Joseph C. Buccilli
P.O. Box 709
Sicklerville, NJ 08081

PART 1

PRESENT FUNCTION DESPITE PAST DYSFUNCTIONS

How can two persons who came from dysfunctional families learn to trust each other?

When those of us who grew up in a dysfunctional family enter into a relationship with someone from a similar background, we both seek immediate and total acceptance! Why is this so?

If we remember that the parents who raised us sent many mixed messages, often behaving in ways that were physically, emotionally, and verbally contradictory, then it becomes easy to see why we may remain confused in our efforts to build a healthy relationship with another person, even years after leaving our parental home.

Some of us well into adulthood are as confused as ever about whom we can safely trust.

As an adult child of an alcoholic (ACOA) myself, in order to learn to trust my wife, I had to work first on trusting myself.

In the beginning whenever we would share our thoughts, I would find myself reacting instead of responding — seeking to overwhelm her with logic (my strong suit), instead of interacting with her on the basis of our emotions. As time went on, I found the courage to share my feelings more openly, yet she was often confused by my behavior, which she saw as impulsive and overreactive.

One of the reasons that our relationship is more mutually satisfying today is that I have taken the time to identify my feelings and allow myself to truly feel them. I had verbalized them before, but now I deal with my feelings in ways that allow both of us to experience a "win/win" situation.

Did you ever stop to think that the heart of T-R-U-S-T is that small but very powerful word, US?

I have slowly learned not to let my past complicate, confuse, or sabotage my — and our — present.

One especially important focus in the process of trust-building for anyone is to recognize that coming to trust is a slow journey, with some smooth times, some temporary delays, and as many detours along the way as are necessary for us to reach the goal.

TO THINK ABOUT:

- ✦ My partner seems to sabotage my trust. How do I know that I can trust him/her?

- ✦ How do I respond to my partner when we're together?

- ✦ Which of my "hidden" feelings have I identified?

- ✦ How do I verbalize these feelings after I recognize them?

- ✦ How are these newly awakened feelings received?

- ✦ Do I allow my toxic habits to get in the way of my need to be close to another?

- ✦ Do my behaviors confuse my partner? How?

If neither of us knew a good relationship growing up, how can we have one together now?

People who were subjected to unhealthy parenting adopted survival methods in order to make it through. Generally we either learned to cope with life's challenges in safer and healthier ways, or else we made no effort to cope at all.

No relationship is a success or failure from its very start. Relationships are about the process of human bonding.

Even though a child did not get the early nurturing he or she needed, the same individual in adulthood can commit personally to making all future relationships healthy ones.

The way to do that is to first "check our own baggage" — the old stuff we're dragging with us from the family we grew up in — before attempting to create an intimate relationship with another person. We "dump that baggage" by reaching out to another person — a therapist, a friend, a sponsor — and discussing the messages we absorbed as we were growing up, messages which we may not even consciously remember. Little by little, we can learn to put new, healthy messages in place of the old toxic ones.

Then, once we feel ready to give our energies to creating a relationship, we seek a partner with whom we can share, someone we can be vulnerable with who will not use our vulnerability against us — in other words, someone who will not dominate, exploit, or abuse us.

Typically, we encounter problems when we begin to try to establish such a relationship. What are some of them?

1. An extreme desire on the part of one person to be healed or protected, which can lead to an unequal, dependent relationship.

2. Getting involved in relationships because we are in search of something, but we don't know what.

3. Expecting a partner to read our minds. When he or she is unable to do so, we feel let down and allow the relationship to fall apart.

4. A desire for complete, mutual emotional support, discounting those unavoidable periods of emotional overload when life's pressures make that impossible.

5. Overprotectiveness toward another that prevents the partner from experiencing the full, normal consequences of their behavior and choices.

6. Becoming too comfortable in our roles and the stage of development of our relationship, thus failing to grow as individuals.

7. Refusing to support a partner's development into the mature person he or she can be, because we feel threatened by the prospect of different expectations.

Reflecting on these various obstacles can help us to discover our own solutions and strategies that lead to healthier relationships and more fulfilling lives.

TO THINK ABOUT:

✦ How do I cope with my own internal conflicts over events of the past?

- Have I identified my "excess" emotional baggage?
- What am I really afraid of?
- Have I dealt with my fear of abandonment?
- By which ways am I growing out from under the baggage of my past family situations?

How can parents who grew up in dysfunctional families learn to bring up healthy kids?

Some of us have been so traumatized that we have settled into a cycle of self-victimization, long after the initial traumas are past. Many of us go through life expecting to be let down or hurt, and when those expectations are fulfilled, we then believe either that we deserved it, or that we couldn't have done any better.

Then there are those of us who survived our past victimization and transcended our injuries to become survivors, those who continue seeking to remain open to new thinking and innovative guidance. If we choose it, this path is open to every one of us.

What are some of these survivors' secrets that help them raise healthy families?

1. Affirmations: "Just because I was brought up in a family where there was dysfunction doesn't mean that I am damaged goods."

2. Helping our kids to see us as role models of effective living. Such parents learn not to place their children in "lose/lose" or even "win/lose" situations, but always to provide "win/win" situations.

3. Demonstrating the value of healthy dialogue — that we can still love each other while agreeing to disagree, in an atmosphere of mutual respect. Healthy families allow diverse points of view, yet no one uses his or her viewpoint to victimize another.

4. Learning to gently parent ourselves. Even if we were not parented in ways that prepared us for the joys and responsibilities of parenthood, we can learn to nurture ourselves before undertaking to parent and nurture children.

5. Allowing my own "inner child" to communicate with my children — not by getting into power struggles with them, but by being able to play, talk, and even argue "nice."

6. Refusing to beat up on ourselves for our mistakes. Rather, we can appreciate and benefit from our missteps, as we learn to be in the world.

7. Not just giving directions, but also taking directions. Sometimes as parents we become too rigid and forget that we, too, are human and teachable. Our children can be our teachers, if we will allow them to be.

8. Letting our children see that we are human and we have feelings and needs. Giving them opportunities to respond in appropriate ways helps to produce compassionate kids.

TO THINK ABOUT:

✦ How do I halt the arguments that pit me against my partner?

✦ Have I identified past injuries that keep me stuck in a victim role?

- What would make for an emotional win/win situation for me?

- How can I put this win/win attitude into practice in my own life and into my relationship with my children?

- What have I learned from my partner and my children today?

If I'm seen as the imperfect one in the family, how can I stop feeling inferior to the others?

The members of all families have differing talents and skills. No talent is better than another, no skill more important than any other. The individuals in all families will naturally differ in intelligence, beauty, or attributes such as athletic ability. And that's okay, because each person has his or her own special gifts.

There are those who make excellent accountants and those who are cut out to be artists. You may be a fine soccer player; I may be good at writing books. That is just the way life works out.

But how do we overcome this mind-set of feeling "less than" another person?

One way is by seeking out and being with people who value us and accept us for who we are. If there are those who always compare us to someone else, it may be better for our spiritual growth to let those people alone.

The key is refusing to buy into the process of comparison, recognizing that *each one of us born into this world is unique.* No other person exactly like you, no other person exactly like me has ever yet been born — not even an identical twin.

When we were young, perhaps our parents were unable to help us value our own talents and originality. Perhaps the dominant culture continues to see us as "odd" or different. But a great part of the task of self-discovery has to do with identifying our unique aptitudes — whatever gives worth and meaning to our lives — and coming to value those special things about ourselves.

How tiresome it would be if we were all exactly alike! If everyone looked like a movie star, or everyone was intellectually brilliant, those qualities would lose their charm, for they would no longer be unique.

You might begin overcoming your feelings of being "less than" by reflecting about your qualities that people outside your family compliment you on. What do people seek you out for? What activities do you find fulfilling and enjoy sharing with others?

You and I — every one of us — is a valuable person, created by a loving God. Perhaps you might consider asking God to help you see what it is that is most valuable in yourself.

TO THINK ABOUT:

- ✦ What in me makes me feel "less than/more than" another?
- ✦ What are my strong qualities?
- ✦ What types of people do I seek to be with?
- ✦ Why do these relationships endure?

Why has my sibling (or other relative) become a stranger?

The reality of life is that either people grow together, or else they grow apart. The moving apart happens when one person is ready to grow and one person is not. This same dynamic happens all over the place — in marriages, families, organizations, friendships, all sorts of relationships and systems.

However much you may want a close relationship with a brother or sister or some other relative, that person will always have his or her own agenda, which may not correspond in any way to your own.

We all have different priorities. Priorities can empower us or disable us. In recovery, because you and I have placed our first priority on healing, we have to work at resisting the pressures tempting us to stay unhealed.

Sometimes in recovery we are so excited about our new way of living that we "talk program" in ways that tend to make others in our life feel left out. Self-inventory is useful when this happens. If we see that we've been doing this, we can make amends by telling the other person, "My life has new meaning and fulfillment, and I just want to share it with everybody. I need you to tell me if I'm not doing it in ways you can appreciate and share."

If I am recovering from the influence of controlling persons who would like to keep me unhealed, or those who only liked me before I moved into recovery living, it's vitally important to remember that healthy relationships don't need control and don't depend on one person being unhealthy. Healthy relationships create trust and mutual respect between individuals.

If your estranged relative sees over the long run that

your life truly has become happier and more serene, it may suggest that such a state of mind is also possible for him or her. Be patient, respecting the other person's timetable. You may be surprised what you can share with other family members over the long haul.

TO THINK ABOUT:

- Do I relate to my siblings now as I did in the past?
- What are my hopes for the future of our relationships?
- What makes me aware that our relationship is a growing one?
- Have I identified those with whom I'd like a closer relationship?

Why is it that our family get-togethers are a kind of "Dysfunction on Parade"?

Where was the dysfunction when you were growing up? It was in the home you grew up in! How many persons from that original family have made the effort and done the hard work to change the patterns of the past? Chances are, not many.

And so whenever members of that original family come together, most of those present probably will not have made much progress in letting go of old roles and old behaviors.

Or suppose you are recovering from a trauma that occurred in a particular setting, around particular people other than your family. Naturally, whenever you go back to that setting or those people, you will feel the old feelings that accompanied the original trauma.

It's up to you to decide whether you want to replay these old "videos" or not. If you decide you do not want to be part of ongoing family dysfunction, your get-togethers can be simple — five minutes, "Hello" and "Good-bye." Or you can limit the contact to a brief phone call now and again. You can send a letter stating, "At this time I cannot come." Such a statement is quite complete — nothing further required.

Please don't misunderstand. Family is important!! And family can put the pressure on in ways no one else knows how to do.

Even so, you must figure out if there is a hidden agenda where you're concerned. Is the hidden agenda whether you are there or not there for the family, or there or not there for the dysfunction?

If you see the "Dysfunction on Parade," the choice is

yours to say and do something, in your own way, that sends the message, "I prefer not to be there so long as dysfunction is running the show."

TO THINK ABOUT:

- How do I divorce myself from the dysfunction but not the family at these family get-togethers?

- Do I spend time afterward evaluating what has happened and planning how I will respond the next time we gather?

- Have I set my own priorities before I attend one of these family gatherings?

- What are my priorities?

Can I get over thinking that the real test of our marriage is surviving family get-togethers?

Of course you can! What possible reason is there for me to carry the dysfunction of my old family household, which may be miles away, into my own partnership and my new household?

Dysfunctional families that are not recovering are said to be "enmeshed," which means that they continue their old behaviors and old interconnections regardless of how sick it may make those who take part.

Healing families, on the other hand, learn to release the emotional bonds that have enmeshed them in these toxic connections.

If you do choose to attend family functions, talk it over ahead of time with your spouse and identify what it is about these gatherings that each of you enjoys and what it is about them that each of you dislikes. Then make a commitment to honor your own and your partner's feelings, if you decide to go.

Once you have done that, you can participate in the parts you enjoy and appreciate, yet separate yourself from any conversation that feels unhelpful. You can detach yourself from activities or interactions you don't like and go home when you — not they — choose! You'll be surprised how liberating such a course of action can be.

If your marriage is being tested by such externals as this, then you must call upon your internal strengths in order to be comfortable with your choice not to attend, or if you do attend, your resolve to come through such get-togethers unscathed.

TO THINK ABOUT:

- How do I show that I am one with my partner and not allied with my own or the partner's family?

- What messages from our family of origin can we use to strengthen our new relationship?

- Which petty struggles are not worth our attention?

Can I forgive another person, move beyond the original event emotionally, and still not feel guilty about not wanting to be in relationship with the person who injured me?

I may know that I need to forgive another person, yet I do not want to be around that person. Can I stay away from him/her and not feel guilty about it?

You do not have to be with a person to forgive that person! Forgiveness is something that happens within your own mind and heart.

The associated issue is about moving beyond the painful past emotionally. To do that, we can learn to let go of guilt around our choice not to be with the person or persons who caused our pain.

One of the keys is learning to live in the present — acknowledging that you are not living with that person now. As a consequence of the separation, you are therefore able to practice, little by little, letting go of the psychic wounds the other person inflicted upon you.

Continuing to feel guilty is a choice. If you really are sorry about something you did or did not do, the proper approach is to make amends. If you acted on your best inner guidance and would make the same choice again, then guilt is neither necessary or appropriate.

Sometimes we confuse our feelings of sadness with feelings of guilt. It's okay to be sad that a relationship has disappointed us, or been destroyed. If it was a sick relationship, however, health and recovery demand that it fall away. So why feel guilty about its disappearance?

An approach many of us use to arrive at forgiveness without falling back into guilt or recurrent enmeshment is praying for the other person and praying for our relationship to that person to be transformed.

TO THINK ABOUT:

- ✦ In which ways have I grieved and let go of my losses?
- ✦ Have I identified the specifics of the injuries?
- ✦ Have I allowed the scars to heal?
- ✦ Have I forgiven myself?
- ✦ What have I learned from this?
- ✦ What do I still feel guilty about?
- ✦ Do I still need to ask for forgiveness?
- ✦ What are my expectations when asking for forgiveness?
- ✦ What happens if I don't get an immediate pardon?

PART 2

THE HOW-TO OF MAKING BOUNDARIES

How can I really reach or touch another person who's been wounded and is therefore afraid of intimacy?

All of us want to feel lovable and approachable. We all want to know that we can love and approach others. Yet from early life we children from dysfunctional families were often told to come close, while the body language of our caretakers or parents sent the message, "Stay away."

If I come from an alcoholic or otherwise dysfunctional family, in order to touch another person or allow another person to touch me, I need to learn about boundaries. My approach, or yours, can never succeed if it feels invasive or threatening in any way.

We can also learn to notice and respect the signals the other person gives. Rather than rushing in too soon or too forcefully, if I stand back and observe until the other person gives me an inviting signal of some kind, I will know when he or she is ready to be approached.

With young children, standing back quietly while modeling approachability often produces a positive response in the child, whereas rushing in with overwhelming embraces and exclamations may have the opposite effect. And those of us who grew up in invasive families often respond like small children, if we fear we are about to be overwhelmed.

Communication happens in talking, in listening, in observing body language, in interacting according to our needs and wants, and in respecting another person's boundaries.

We can use our skills to identify another's behavior,

rather than reacting to the other's behavior. In the same way, we can give another person signals that we are ready for a little more closeness, when the time is right.

TO THINK ABOUT:

- ✦ As a child, how did I respond to others when they greeted me at family gatherings?

- ✦ Did I ever become comfortable at identifying who I like and who I do not like?

- ✦ Do I truly know where I set my own boundaries?

- ✦ How do I show my real boundaries?

- ✦ Am I clear about how much personal closeness to another I can handle?

How much can another be allowed to take from me?

In framing my relationship with another person, the healthy focus is on what I am willing to give. In order to give to someone else, I must have *something* to give, whether it be love, respect, or a service. And if I find myself in a situation where I am endlessly giving and endlessly being taken from, then I have the right to decide when enough is enough.

How will I know when enough is enough? If we listen to our guts, all of us naturally know.

Being able to say "Enough is enough" only happens when I come to believe that I deserve not to be exploited or treated with disrespect. It is okay to stop being a doormat!

There are times when we know enough is enough yet still feel guilty about saying so. This guilt is nothing more than an emotional indicator of a dilemma. The self-respecting part of ourself says an emphatic "No," yet the self-abasing part keeps saying, "Just a little more."

We feel uncomfortable because we are changing to healthier behaviors, and change is always uncomfortable and unfamiliar at first.

How do I handle guilt? One way would be to just keep on walking around with my guilt until that guilt turns to shame, which turns into self-destructive attitudes.

Or I can talk about the guilt. If I'm in a 12-Step program, I can talk about it to others in the fellowship including my sponsor, if I'm in counseling I can talk to my counselor, I can talk to God, and I can cry about it.

And eventually I can let my guilt go, knowing that I have refused to submit to another's manipulations and done what is best for my own spiritual growth.

TO THINK ABOUT:

- ✦ Have I identified those times in my life when I felt that "enough was enough"? What were they?
- ✦ How did others respond to my decision?
- ✦ Whom did I seek out to strengthen me in my decision?
- ✦ What am I really able to give to another?
- ✦ Do I practice talking from my heart, my head, or my soul?

How can my partner and I be equals in our relationship, instead of always taking turns being "parent" and "child"?

Some of us get into relationships seeking unconsciously to be parented or to parent. If I feel a need to be parented and try to put my spouse into the role of a parent, one of two things will happen: he/she will either accept the role and parent me, which isn't healthy for either of us, or else she/he will reject the role, leaving us with a very uneasy relationship.

It *seems* easier to accept the desired role than it would be to relinquish the role and learn better coping skills. In the long run, however, the easier way is to grow out of *all* roles and thereby avoid lifelong chronic emotional pain around these issues.

An adult person who continues to need another adult person to parent him or her has some challenging work to do around issues of old family baggage. And one who continues to accept being the "parent" for another capable adult has similarly challenging work to do.

We know we are on the right path when we can give up all our roles to become partners and equals — to become our truest selves.

TO THINK ABOUT:

✦ What parenting skills do I have?

- How do I use them in mutually satisfying and healthy ways?

- Can I feel child-like while remaining an adult?

- What role do I adopt at least 50% of the time?

- During which life event or crisis have we switched our family roles?

If one partner starts to heal, how can the other partner keep from feeling abandoned?

If I happen to be in the process of healing from past wounds created by my original family or some other trauma, and if I want any relationship that I am in to last, that relationship must also partake of the healing.

Healing doesn't happen in a vacuum. Healing is not just personal; it's interpersonal. When any one of us changes, all significant others in our life must react or respond to that change.

If the person who is healing and changing comes across as a know-it-all or acts superior to a relationship partner, self-inventory is the appropriate move.

If I am the healing one, I need to share not just my words but also my healing attitudes. If I am now able to feel loved and accepted, I can share those feelings with you by letting you know that you are also loved and accepted.

On the other hand, if you came out of a relationship where you felt abandoned by a partner who "outgrew" you, you will be dragging your own old baggage along and worrying that I may be about to outgrow you as well.

Because I can't read your mind, I will need you to tell me about any feelings of abandonment that may have cropped up in this present relationship, and where they came from.

Those of us who feel abandoned come out of situations where sometimes it was "lose/lose" or sometimes "win/lose." The whole process of healing is about creating "win/win" situations, and it takes both of us to make it succeed.

TO THINK ABOUT:

- ✦ Have I identified the origin of my own wounds?
- ✦ What have been my own expectations for healing?
- ✦ Have I identified past relationships that I have outgrown?
- ✦ What am I continuing to mature through at this time?
- ✦ Have I identified the abandonment issues in my life?

How can I become comfortable with letting another person help me?

Accepting help becomes more comfortable as I become more open to others.

What is it about accepting another person's help that I fear? I may fear that I will accept the help and then be abandoned. I may fear that I will lose control (a "biggie" for ACOAs). Or I may fear that I am not worthy of another person's help.

Behind my unwillingness to accept another person's help may even be a secret arrogance — a self-centered refusal to allow the other person the joy of helping or giving.

In any of these cases, as I learn to take small steps and gradually allow myself to trust, I know that with time and practice it will become easier to accept another person's help and any gifts she or he has to offer.

Instead of letting our fears dominate our thinking, we can use those fears as stepping-stones on which to stand as we pull down the defensive "walls" we have built around ourselves.

We all want to be social and get together with other people, yet each of us harbors some fear that sharing something of ourselves with another person may give that person something to use against us. We may even fear that if we let people know a little about us, they will want to know everything, even our darkest secrets.

Yet we are only as sick as our sickest secrets. Some of us have allowed our secrets to hold such power over us that they become like gigantic mountains — mountains that we keep trying to scale, yet all we can do is to continue sliding back down.

Once I become able, I'll accept everything about who I am, even my secrets and my fears, and that's great!

And when I can name my secrets and my fears and share them with another trustworthy person, my secrets and fears will begin to lose their power over me.

TO THINK ABOUT:

- What are the limits of my comfort zone?
- Where have I hidden my secrets?
- Did I ever share a secret and have it used against me?
- Have I healed from this offense yet?
- Where is that relationship today?

How can I know I'm good enough, if my partner has impossibly high standards?

Some of us base our entire lives on acceptance by certain key persons. And some of our relationship partners have impossibly high standards. We may try to reach those high standards, striving ceaselessly to live at the level expected of us, even when it's a level we are not comfortable with.

If I grew up in a family where no one ever affirmed or validated me, I may always be seeking affirmation or validation from others yet never finding it. Or I may be constantly trying to validate or affirm myself, struggling to prove my worth and demonstrate that I'm "good enough." I may continue this struggle longer than anyone coming out of a healthier family background would tolerate.

What's the solution? A basic one is to fill my life with people who accept me, people I am comfortable with, people who appreciate me just as I am. I can find these people in recovery meetings, my faith community, other families, and at work and play.

I realize that I will never find happiness as long as I continue trying to base my identity on some other person's yardstick, no matter if that person is my partner, another relative, or an employer.

I am the only one who knows whether I am being the person God intended me to be, and if I am doing that, no other person's opinion really matters.

TO THINK ABOUT:

- What types of influence do I allow others to have on me?
- Do I influence others fairly?
- Who are the key people in my life?
- Why is each one of them important to me?
- What personal standards do we use?

Will I lose myself if I try to hold a relationship together, no matter what happens?

Sad to say, many of us would rather be in a bad relationship than no relationship at all, putting ourselves in a "no-win" situation from the start. It's like saying, "I would rather be dragged down the road behind an automobile driven by my lover than walk uneventfully along the sidewalk alone."

It takes tremendous courage to get out of an unfulfilling relationship, but hanging onto it takes an even greater personal toll. Anyone who attempts to keep a toxic relationship going indefinitely will lose a part of his/her own spirit, damage his/her spirituality, and forsake his/her own identity.

The true answer is, "Yes, you will sacrifice yourself if you continue to hang on to a destructive relationship."

Sometimes we have to lose in order to gain: lose the baggage of the past to live wholly and creatively in the present, and lose a destructive relationship in order to be open to a new, constructive one.

TO THINK ABOUT:

- ✦ Do I manifest my own toxicity in the relationship, or is the relationship toxic in itself?

- Can I identify the feelings I had during times in my life when I was alone?

- Did I look for a partner at that time just to fill those needs?

- Do I recognize the factors at work when my relationships work well?

How can I differentiate between supportiveness and codependency?

Problems arise when you or I pair up with another person who has the same difficulty we have in differentiating between supportiveness and codependency.

It's important to surround ourselves with persons who are supportive but who do not overprotect or seek to stifle our individuality. And it's important to be supportive of another person without doing too much for him or her, or seeking to limit her or his personal growth.

How do we know whether the other person is truly supportive? We discover that by making ourself a little bit open and a little bit vulnerable to the other person, and if that person respects our boundaries and is kind to us around our vulnerabilities, we then know that we're being supported in a healthy way. And of course it works the other way, too.

God created us to be neither totally dependent nor totally independent, but primarily interdependent. The healthy balance in all relationships is what matters.

TO THINK ABOUT:

✦ How do I cope with rejection?

✦ What types of emotional/spiritual/physical/ intellectual supports do I seek?

- ✦ Have I identified those who are supportive and those who are codependent in my life?

- ✦ When I show my vulnerable side, what does my partner do?

- ✦ How do I respond to this reaction in him/her?

- ✦ How am I supportive of others? Is it ever too much?

How can I differentiate between independence and distancing?

Sometimes it's hard to tell the difference between independence and distancing.

Distancing is running away. You don't have to run away physically to distance yourself; you can put on a face that gives the impression you are present when, in your mind, you are hundreds of miles away. You can also put on a face that indicates your psychological absence, if you're not in sync with your present company.

Sometimes it's important to distance ourselves from people, places, and things that are toxic to us. We have heard of children whose abuse caused them to distance themselves to the point that multiple personalities formed — a strategy that served their survival, even if it caused great trouble in later life.

Sometimes too much independence isn't good. Human connections, healthy ones, are essential to a good life. It's a very thin line all of us walk in trying to keep our emotional equilibrium.

Some persons by the guidance of their inner natures are quite independent. Yet other seemingly independent persons have become that way as a reaction to some exterior force, rather than as a response to inner guidance.

Our inner guidance comes from faith in God, faith in our parents or other trusted persons, faith in ourselves. Spiritual growth comes through practices that strengthen our inner guidance and allow us to stop overvaluing the opinions of others, while staying open to human acceptance and support.

TO THINK ABOUT:

- How do I display my need for independence to my partner, my family, and my friends?
- What are my nonverbal cues to my partner when I start to distance myself?
- Have I identified the underlying feelings?
- What motivates me during these times?
- As a child, how did I respond to similar situations?
- Do I respond the same way now as an adult?

How can I tell the difference between your "stuff" and my "stuff"?

Maybe it's about our stuff! If I'm in a problematic relationship, the problems don't belong to one or the other — the problems belong to both.

A lot of what affects a relationship has to do with things that happened way-back-then and haven't yet been worked through. All that stuff plays a part in what's going on now.

A relationship is about working toward a common goal. So if there are times when you think, "I'm okay, he's the one that needs fixing," or times when I think, "I'm okay, she's the one that's screwed up," our task at that point is to do something that will move both of us to a better place to look for solutions.

Ultimatums aren't generally helpful until everything else has been tried. What may be helpful at first is a statement something like this one: "I feel uncomfortable with the way things are going, and I want us to talk about this."

We will generally benefit more if both of us put the emphasis on listening rather than being heard, and it has to work both ways.

Relationships are about the long-term process of change. "Your stuff versus my stuff" is a short-term, limited approach to a relationship. Relationships are about "us," long-term. As we seek to reach a peaceful place for both of us to be in, the most useful question is, "What will be best for the relationship over the long haul?"

It may also be helpful to look for patterns — the things about this situation and about each other that caused us to wind up in this relationship. Are we doing something we did somewhere else before? Did it work then? If not, why not? What is similar in the present set-up? What is different? What can we do differently from what we did before?

Once we have looked at these patterns, even if we leave the relationship, we will learn and become able to change our ways of responding to others. That way we will not be doomed to repeat the same self-defeating pattern.

TO THINK ABOUT:

- What kind of "stuff" do I bring with me to my relationships?
- Do I scapegoat others when I feel myself caught up in a power struggle?
- Have I identified ways in which my partner and I respond to our disagreements?
- Do we stick to the solutions we agree upon?
- How well do I respond to ultimatums?

In an alcoholic or otherwise dysfunctional family, is the most "together" person a good role model?

We who grew up in dysfunctional families have internalized certain out-of-balance coping skills in order to survive. And until each of us has done the vital personal work that leads to self-discovery and self-acceptance, what we present to the world is really a "false face" — one more wall of defense against feelings. As long as that's going on, our insides don't match our outsides.

One of these "false faces" is the "perfect" son or daughter, the family "hero," the achiever, the strong one in the family, the one everyone admires or wants to be like. This is the person who strives to show the world that someone in such a family can do things right.

Yet there is no perfect person. Looks are deceiving! After such a "perfect" person becomes an adult, the world may not recognize this man's or this woman's anxieties, fears, or defenses, but you can be sure they exist. Everyone has anxieties, fears, and defenses. That's just a part of being fully human.

If I emulate another person, copying the way that person dresses or talks or walks in order to feel strong myself, I am not really trusting myself. I am simply putting my trust in another's false face, another's mask.

How much better to work for my own personal progress, instead of trying to copy the seeming "perfection" I think I see in another. Following my own inner guidance of what is true for me will help me be the best person I can become.

Of course, there are certain admirable characteristics we can all cultivate, such as honesty, open-mindedness, being worthy of another person's trust, being responsible. Those are qualities each of us can strive for, because they are authentic and represent the nobler part of what it means to be truly human.

TO THINK ABOUT:

✦ Do I know the roles I have played and continue to play?

✦ What characteristics have I internalized that make me feel more human and alive?

✦ Who was the "together" person in my family?

✦ How does this person respond to life's challenges today?

✦ As a teen-ager, did I adopt peer-group attitudes, or did I formulate a strong sense of myself?

How can I fit in with my original family and my in-laws? Do I have to? Do I really want to?

When the family system that includes in-laws is dysfunctional, there's plenty of second-guessing. Both you and your significant other have to be willing to discuss and decide between yourselves how important these original family systems are to the two of you.

Dysfunctionality is all about lack of boundaries and confusing, inauthentic priorities. You and your partner will be wise to identify the confusion and the bewildering boundaries, then talk through your issues around the subject without getting into power struggles with each other.

At different places and different times, all of us fit in or don't fit in. Sometimes it's healthiest not to fit in, if we've been trying to adapt to a toxic relational system.

Pleasing everybody and meeting everyone's expectations at the same time is virtually impossible. This is why it's so important to know our own priorities.

If you really want your present family to be an extension of your original family or your partner's original family, you will have to decide together as a couple whether you're willing to pay the price to fit into those family systems.

Whatever you decide, remember that you and your partner have grown and changed while the original family may have remained the same old rigid, closed system. If you go back to family get-togethers expecting different results, you are setting yourself up for disappointments and what feel like relational failures.

Go if you can, fit in if you can. But if you are in the process of healing old wounds and attempting to break out of toxic family roles, you don't have to keep on putting yourself into situations where you'll always be reminded of those old wounds or your old role.

Serenity comes when we can be ourselves and live out of our own expectations, rather than trying to fit into the unsuitable expectations of others.

TO THINK ABOUT:

✦ What makes it possible for me to talk about my family dysfunction with my partner?

✦ How have I stopped bringing the old "junk" into our new household?

✦ Have I identified my expectations vs. my partner's expectations around family gatherings?

✦ Have we expressed our own healing process in ways that keep both of us above external family criticism?

How do I get inner permission to be myself when I'm with them and avoid adapting to their "stuff"?

If the circumstances of your early life caused you to become a people-pleaser so that others would like you or wouldn't hurt you, until you recognize this pattern and become able to let go of it, you will constantly be manipulated by other people in your life.

We become comfortable being ourselves once we decide that we don't have to have other people like us or accept us. When we accept ourselves, other people's acceptance or lack of it no longer matters. If they like and accept us, well and good, but if they don't, we can live without it.

Every human being is either in the process of growing or stuck in not-growing. Everything really boils down to that. If you have reached the point of letting go of most of your old emotional baggage, your life will be the richer for it. But don't expect others who chose not-growing to applaud. What matters is that you have recovered your soul.

TO THINK ABOUT:

- ✦ What do I know about myself?
- ✦ Am I myself only when I'm alone, or can I be myself while interacting with others?
- ✦ What happens to me if I choose to stay within a dysfunctional role?

Why is it that every time I go onto their turf, I submit to an inquisition? How do I stop it?

Some people will not allow another person to be who he or she is, but seek to control or manipulate. This may be what you go up against when you venture back into "their" territory, if you find yourself facing an inquisition, or the "third degree." In this situation, it's hard at first to know how to stop the uncomfortable treatment we receive.

Even in families, some people are predators. Not all predators will behave in physically abusive ways toward those they seek to control, but they may behave in mentally and emotionally abusive ways.

You must first decide whether this is what is happening when you get the inquisition. If so, then you must say to your inquisitor, in your own way, "I feel attacked when you treat me this way, and I don't like it. I want to spend time with you, but if I continue feeling attacked, I will have to leave."

Once again we are dealing with boundaries, with putting-up-with, with allowing. The other person may not even realize he/she is violating your boundaries, if you have never expressed that feeling. If you have simply continued to take it without telling the other person how you feel, you have been giving permission for the behavior to go on.

You have a choice in this situation — whether to continue coming back and allowing the perceived attacks to go on, or whether to say how you feel and stop coming if the other person won't stop the behavior.

It's simpler than you might imagine. We stop this repetitive behavior by not allowing it to continue!

Simple is not the same as easy, however. For many of us, walking away from an uncomfortable situation that involves a family member may be a very difficult thing to do. We've been taught to "be nice," to be polite, not to hurt other people's feelings. Learning to interrupt abusive behavior is a skill we have to work to acquire.

So if you cannot stop the offensive behavior cold, you can stop it by degrees. If a person continues putting you down after you've expressed yourself clearly about it, then it's up to you to find new friends, new "family," new people to associate with. As you gradually phase out the time you were spending with predators, you will find your emotional needs being fulfilled by the healthier, more accepting circle of friends with whom you surround yourself.

TO THINK ABOUT:

- ✦ Have I decided in advance what I will share with them?
- ✦ For what reason have I been compromising my values?
- ✦ Have I decided that I'm healthy and they're not, or is it that they're healthy and I'm not?
- ✦ Am I actively seeking new "family" and friends as I get healthier?

How can I protect my kids from the others at our family gatherings?

You will not be able to protect your kids from others at family get-togethers *while you are there.* The protection comes about through the communication that is already in place between you and your children, the communication that was set up long before you ever attended a family event.

It may not be that your family or your partner's family actually wants to harm your kids. People do and say harmful things without even knowing what they are about. The rules and expectations in your household will probably not be the same as the rules and values in the larger family system. It's good to let your children know that, pointing out what some of these differences may be.

Talking openly about issues is a hallmark of a healthy recovering family system. Even in the best of circumstances, misunderstandings occur. And when they do, the appropriate action is to talk the matter through. A misunderstanding ignored can take root and grow into dysfunction. A misunderstanding examined and worked through can produce healthy functionality.

Your task is to empower your children to recognize and deal appropriately with the dysfunctional behavior of other people, even when those others are adults. The key is not protection but preparation. You are giving your children the knowledge and coping skills that will make them feel strong and competent in difficult situations, rather than trying to overprotect and fight their battles for them.

TO THINK ABOUT:

- ✦ What do my kids understand about the entire family system?
- ✦ How do I go about talking with my kids about these issues?
- ✦ In what ways have I learned to listen to my kids?
- ✦ In what ways do I cooperate with them?
- ✦ Have I taken the time to recognize my child's responses to our family gatherings?

How can I get over feeling resentful toward a partner who hasn't yet succeeded in healing old-family issues and who behaves as I behaved years ago?

Each of us has an individual timetable for personal growth. If I have made progress in growing emotionally and changing old behaviors, I may find it hard to stand back and watch a partner continue in the old destructive behaviors I used to do. I may even feel resentment about having to watch it happen.

Recovery is not about comparison. It's not a competition to see who gets to the finish line first. Recovery is about sharing, about living my own growth, about being grateful that I have come as far as I have come.

Recovery and adult mature blending-with-others bring responsibilities. So if you are interacting on a daily basis with someone who appears less healthy than you think you may be, you can simply share your own recovery without dictating or manipulating, always seeking to understand the other person, and acting out of compassion for the partner who is not yet fully healed.

TO THINK ABOUT:

✦ Do I listen to what my partner says, even though his/her antics might get me sidetracked?

- What fueled my past resentments?

- Am I actively fueling resentments now?

- How do I respond to issues where I would like to see my partner having made more progress?

- How do I discuss my response with my partner?

- Can I agree to respect the disagreement until a better time for discussing it can be found?

PART 3

HOW TO ACCEPT AND LIKE REALITY IN RELATIONSHIPS

How can I outgrow a "me against the world" attitude?

There are more similarities than differences between human beings. Yet a certain mind-set says, "We always have to be on our guard, we have to keep our defenses up." This is survival thinking, left over from trying to make it in a dysfunctional, addictive, or otherwise abusive family.

That's why it's so important for those of us who come from dysfunctional foundations to avoid dragging our past baggage or damage into the present. It takes so much energy to stay ready to pounce, or dodge, or run and hide! It takes so much energy to keep up the "walls" we have built to protect ourselves.

For people like you and me, the focus must be, not "me against the world," but "me in the world," a world that abounds in opportunities for growth and moments of beauty and grace.

Human beings by nature are extremely insecure. Hence we must set ourselves to foster security based on a solid foundation. Attitude has a lot to do with feeling secure — whether we habitually see the glass as half empty, or teach ourselves to see it half full. Attitudes *can* be changed. We can keep on saying, "I told you they were out to get me," or we can accept any crisis as an opportunity for growth. We can look for the lesson in things that befall us, seeking the gifts in every moment of the day.

Once we find the courage to let down some of those walls we built to protect ourselves from the world, we discover that while the walls kept the world out, they were also keeping us in!

When I stop seeing myself as the object of a cosmic

conspiracy, when I stop spending all my energies to protect myself, I discover that I have abundant energy to invest in joyous, positive, creative life pursuits.

TO THINK ABOUT:

- ✦ Who am I?
- ✦ Who and what fills my "inner spring"?
- ✦ How do I stay open to the lessons of life?
- ✦ Where have I built up my walls and defenses?
- ✦ Where do my creative pursuits lie?

How can I get over seeing and expecting everything to be always romantic?

I hope I will never get over seeing everything as romantic! Instead, I just keep redefining romance.

Romance is not only about the play; romance is also about the foreplay and the afterplay. In a relationship, sex is a part of it, but sexuality is the majority of it — male sexuality, female sexuality, human sexuality, spiritual sexuality, emotional sexuality, intimacy.

So the question is not how to get over expecting everything to always be romantic, but rather, how to succeed at keeping it romantic!

There are so many ways of going about it. Romance is not just in the boudoir or the bedroom. Romance is in the car, in the living room, in the dining room, in the kitchen. Romance is in *people,* and it's up to us to continue to kindle those romantic feelings and to share our love, not just our sexual desires, with the right partner.

Love means knowing when to speak and when to listen. Love means knowing when to share and when to recognize that everything isn't always the way it seems in the movies.

Romance can be helping your partner with the vacuuming, or carrying a folding chair out to the garage to keep your partner company while she works on the car.

Love is not a question of getting over the honeymoon — it's a question of extending and enlarging the honeymoon until it becomes the totality of the relationship.

TO THINK ABOUT:

- ✦ How do I satisfy my need for romance?
- ✦ How do I keep the "fires" burning inside me and my soulmate?
- ✦ What are my connections between romance and intimacy?
- ✦ Do I practice listening to my partner?

Is it possible that I can hide my addiction(s), even from myself?

No one can hide an addiction from other people forever, nor can I forever hide an addiction from myself.

I may have adopted coping mechanisms that help me to conceal the truth, for a while. You may have been able to put on a front that keeps others from seeing, for a time, how obsessed you are with another person or thing, or how compulsive your behavior may have become.

As a counselor, I have worked with hundreds of women and men who knew from an early age that their drinking, drugging, or other obsessive behaviors were destructive to themselves and to others. They knew that these behaviors would eventually lead them to a life crisis.

Growing up in a dysfunctional family, most of us bought into the myth, "It's not that bad." We learned to minimize unpleasant things that were happening, even to the point of denying the reality of our own life experience.

It isn't pleasant to admit that we have addictions of our own — tobacco, alcohol, other drugs, gambling, overeating, sex, pornography, relationships, shopping, seeking to control — whatever stands in the way of being our healthiest selves, whatever gets in the way of our best relationship with God and with other human beings.

We don't consciously hide our addictions. We simply minimize them, rationalize about them, color them, or overcompensate for them. It's a way of making believe, of trusting in "magical" thinking to protect me and my family from the impact of my addictions.

If you want to know whether your addictive behavior

is really hidden, ask the person closest to you to give you an honest answer. I'm grateful today to have caring persons in my life who can mirror my imperfections for me and help me to grow.

TO THINK ABOUT:

- ✦ In what ways did I allow my family's obsessions to have power over me?
- ✦ Have I desensitized myself to what was going on then?
- ✦ How did my family respond to a member's obsession?
- ✦ Have I identified my own dependencies?

I'm an adult now, out of my parents' house. How can I leave pretense behind me to become real?

When we are young, if someone in our family manifests addictive or abusive or even unenlightened behavior, we declare to ourselves, "When I grow up, I'm not going to be anything like X," or Y, or whoever the person is.

We think we can't wait until we become the parent — the father, the mother — because we know we'll never treat others the way we ourselves were treated.

Sounds easy, doesn't it? Curiously, it is not so easy. Breaking an unhealthy relationship cycle doesn't happen just because we want to break it. No matter how hard we may try as adults to do differently, consciously, subconsciously, or unconsciously, we perpetuate the patterns we knew when we were growing up.

While living under another person's roof all of us engage in some pretenses, particularly if things in that household are not going well. Some of us pretend everything's OK when things are really terrible. Some of us simply withdraw. Some of us behave in ways that distract attention from the problem — for example, making people laugh. Some of us act out, calling attention to the problem by our hostile or rebellious behavior. A rebel-victim may even be victimized again for calling attention to the family's problems, in addition to being punished for specific anti-social acts.

Many young men and women escape their parental homes in various ways: military service, early marriage, becoming pregnant, physically running away. Others seek the peace in religious life they failed to find at home. Still others wind up in the criminal justice system, only to find they must still live under restrictive rules.

No one who escapes an unhappy home can immediately discard his or her old role in that family's life. If I was the rebel in my first home, I will probably be the rebel in other settings in the future until I learn to recognize that I'm repeating old patterns. If I was one who put up with, I will probably put up with on a continuing basis until some event takes place that I can no longer tolerate.

Some of us, myself included, became helping professionals because we were powerless to help other members of our own families. And yet eventually we too must walk our own road to healing, working our way through family-of-origin issues that have lain dormant, sometimes for many years.

There's a familiar saying, "You can run but you can't hide." We who ran away in some fashion must eventually deal with our feelings about the past if we are to attain healthy, fulfilling lives.

I might try to pretend that I carry no patterns of dysfunctional living with me. Yet if family dysfunction was a part of my past, until I intervene on it, it will continue to affect my present and my future, eventually leading to a life crisis.

It's wisest to accept our life crises gratefully, for they represent opportunities to face old issues, stop the pretense, and recognize that we no longer have to live in victimization. Instead, we can develop newer, life-enhancing coping skills.

TO THINK ABOUT:

- Why does my partner think that I am always judging him/her?

- Do I recognize the skeletons in my own closet?

- What motivates me to endure the pain of looking at my past?

- Have I identified the "rebel" or "victim" behaviors in my family?

- In what ways have I sought to run away from my past?

Why do I long for their love, when I'm not even sure I still want it?

If all families were ideal, we would all love one another and be loved by one another perfectly, forever. But not all families are ideal, and many of us have been damaged in our capacity to give or accept love.

All the same, it's only human to continue to long for love from someone who can give back the best, truest kind.

Love is not love when it has to be pursued or captured. Love is a gift freely given. Love is shared.

Human beings naturally want to be loved by their family, but not all family members can or will respond to that need. And when family members don't respond as we hope, our own love may require us to learn to let go.

Standing back is not always about rejection, and silence is not always about giving up. Silence and standing back can be about giving another person space, if that person needs it at that particular time. When we are in true recovery, we no longer feel uncomfortable about allowing another person his or her space.

Love is sometimes about change, about taking a different direction from the one we've always taken before. The most mature love may require us to let go of the old and worn-out in order to make room for the new.

TO THINK ABOUT:

- What do I want from others?

- What can I give others from my present self-acceptance?

- Can I describe how I give my family love?

- Who in my family does not accept my love?

- How do they respond to me?

- How do I respond to that?

- How have I learned to give them the space they may need?

How can I become willing to see my part in a situation without being afraid to face up to it?

We all have a special part to play in the dramas that make up our lives. At various times, we have played various parts — heroes, villains, supporting roles.

When our relationship to another person changes, even though the outward circumstances may be radically different, the feelings that went along with the relationship may not have undergone the same renewal.

The old "camera" in our eyes and the old "microphones" in our ears are constantly replaying recordings of the past. Many of us try to run away from relationships that seem not to be working — failed marriages, a dysfunctional family of origin, disappointing friendships — but there is no way that either you or I can run away from ourselves. Wherever I go, the repository of all my experiences, all my dreams that were fulfilled and unfulfilled, all my hopes and desires and my joys and my sorrows, goes right along with me. Wherever I go, there I still am!

Any relationship involves more than one person, and every person in it contributes behaviors, words, feelings, and choices to the relationship, for good or for bad. My partner may be contributing elements that are rooted in a painful past, while I may be doing the same thing.

It's important to take responsibility for our own actions and choices, and for their consequences. If I did it, I can't hide from it. And if I failed to do it, that knowledge will be with me wherever I go. I must take a conscientious self-inventory, make amends wherever possible, and then put the matter to rest.

The only constructive alternative to dragging the painful past around with me forever is to learn to live in the present, as gratefully and as fully as possible, one moment at a time, one hour at a time, one day at a time. And when I have learned to live in the present, I will have learned to deal usefully with my past.

Some of us are so traumatized that we settle, at least temporarily, for bad relationships rather than having no relationships at all. And when those relationships bring up old pain, healthy people and those of us in recovery allow that recurring pain to serve as a wake-up call.

If we can say to ourselves, "I have felt this pain before," instead of further revitalizing that pain, we can learn to revitalize the part of ourselves that says, "I am no longer a victim. This doesn't have to hurt me again."

Remaining a victim requires a great deal of energy. So long as we keep replaying those old "tapes" over and over again, we are continuously internalizing their sad message, until they become part and parcel of us. I must accept that one part of me is comfortable with being a victim, but I can also now act to rid myself of the old victim identity.

Even using the word "victim" can help to perpetuate the pain. Rape victims, incest victims, battering victims? Not necessarily so! If you're getting healthy and growing and changing, if you no longer give over your personal power to another, then you are no longer a victim but a *survivor!*

How do I let go of the pain and the victimhood? I do it by sharing that pain with another person or group of persons. I talk it through until I have worked it through.

Out of crisis comes growth. I am a survivor, and that which hasn't killed me has only served to make me strong.

Now it's up to me to play it out, try it out, write it out, or whatever I want to do to get it out. Accepting my part in the solution, the resolution, the self-forgiveness, and the forgiveness of other people is crucial.

My dad told me many years ago that when you live only in the past, craving revenge, you are really digging two graves — one for you and one for the person you want to put into the grave.

I cannot stay in the past with its pain. I must live in the present, grateful for being a survivor, thanking the Higher Power that speaks to my heart: "You are someone special. You matter."

TO THINK ABOUT:

✦ How do I help my partner realize the consequences of his/her impulsive behavior?

✦ Which healing capabilities do I sustain within myself?

✦ Which ones do I share with others?

✦ What do I do with my anger when we start to talk about these things?

✦ Have we set up specific times to talk, and have we identified the specific issues to be discussed?

✦ How well do I cope when my partner brings up the past?

How can I relate in a healthy way to my former partner and the new partner he or she has chosen?

How do you relate to an "old" partner or an "old" spouse, someone you used to be in a relationship with?

It's tricky, especially if there was a high level of negativity accompanying your time together or your parting. We might prefer to have nothing to do with this person, but sometimes it's required of us that we work out a new way to deal with him or her, as well as a new partner of choice. I can best do this by treating my former partner and his/her new partner with respect, dignity, and boundaries.

All of us who grew up in dysfunctional families and later found ourselves in dysfunctional relationships have weak boundaries, or boundaries that are constantly shifting. But if we are growing, this is changing. So, when I encounter a significant person from my past, I will be wise to relate to that person only in the present circumstances of here and now.

As a recovering person, I am guided by my newfound self-respect when I decline to reopen old wounds. I am now taking care of myself in ways that will energize and revitalize me. And in so doing, I also accord the other person and his or her new partner the human respect to which they are entitled.

TO THINK ABOUT:

- Which old "tapes" do I carry into my new relationships?

- Is what I am doing good for me at this time?

- How do I deal with a former partner or that partner's new partner who does not give me the respect I deserve?

- Have we figured out a way to talk about the kids — yours, mine, ours?

How can I be real in relationships without appearing as needy as I feel?

It's part of being human to be needy! However, some of our needs can become obsessive, especially if we were not shown unconditional love in our earliest years. It's important to make sure our needs are appropriate, and it's equally important to get them met in an appropriate fashion.

I can't expect another person to meet my obsessional emotional needs. It's very wearing to constantly try to meet the emotional needs of someone who can never be satisfied regardless of how much is given.

There is an answer to too-neediness, however. When I recognize that I have been asking too much of another person in terms of my emotional needs, that awareness can lead me in either of two directions. I can remain overly needy and risk losing the other person's respect, or I can begin to satisfy some of my emotional needs in healthier ways.

Self-examination is always the place to begin when relationships are not going smoothly. We ask ourselves what we want from a relationship, what we are afraid of losing, and what we have to give to another person. We also ask ourselves if it's reasonable to expect just one human being to supply all our needs. Almost always, the answer is no.

Many of us have been in relationships in which all our needs were focused on another person. When this happens, we lose touch with our own recovering self, our own healthy inner guidance. If I recognize that this is what I have been doing, I can try to identify my needs and then, little by little, bit by bit, satisfy some of them in ways that do not tax or strain the relationship.

Changing the ways we get our needs met can come about through our reading, our praying, our support networks, and our new ways of interacting with other people.

The only thing that grows well in darkness is a mushroom! As a person, I do not grow well unless I have a variety of others in my life who can help with my needs to be accepted, loved, and cared for. It works like this: first, I need me, and then I need parts of other people, and then other people need parts of me. It's all about interdependence again. All of us have much of value to share with others in our world, but because of the 2% or the 3% that we aren't willing to share, we stop short of sharing the 97% or the 98% that could make such a difference to someone else.

The 12-Step programs teach that the only way to keep something valuable is by sharing it, the only way to grow something is by nurturing it, and the only way that I can truly be me is by sharing myself with other people who are also seeking to become their own best selves.

TO THINK ABOUT:

- Have I identified my age-appropriate needs? My role-appropriate needs? My status-appropriate needs?
- What are my partner's needs?
- What steps do I take to get my needs met?
- How do I respond when my needs are not met?
- Am I asking too much? Am I not asking enough?

How can I recognize and choose a partner who naturally loves?

Recognizing a potential partner who naturally loves is not really terribly difficult, but we often go looking for it because we hope that another person "will make it happen for us." We hope there will be something external we can detect — a clue that tells us, "This is someone who will do all the love part for you, who will enable you to flow right into love and keep it wonderful and perfect forever, and who will help you feel totally filled up and enchanted always!" Some order!

The reality is rather different. It takes a lot of work to really love someone without always expecting the other person to feel totally loving toward you at every moment, or expecting that you will feel the same way at every moment toward him or her. You can seek to be a naturally loving person yourself in the relationship, allowing and inviting the other person to respond as best she or he can.

TO THINK ABOUT:

- Have I specifically identified my own intimacy needs?
- What do I want in a loving relationship?
- What will I settle for?
- Does my partner fill my needs?
- Do I make allowances if my partner cannot meet all my expectations?

SPECIAL SECTIONS

20 Habits That Make A Healthy Relationship

1 ***Having fun together.*** Sometimes it's hard for those of us who come from troubled families to allow ourselves to have fun. We may even think we don't deserve to have any fun! Yet the ability to play satisfies an important human need. And playing can ultimately be more important spiritually than unremitting work.

2 ***Loving each other freely.*** We can and should ask for what we need and want in our relationship, but if our relationship is a healthy one, we give love wholeheartedly, accepting each other as is, with no qualifications or limitations.

3 ***Willingness to work through conflicts.*** We can ignore conflicts, hoping they will go away (they rarely do), we can state our position and never budge (discounting the other person's point of view and robbing ourselves of a chance to learn), or we can discuss our conflicts and work them through. Then both of us have an opportunity to grow as we learn to trust each other to find a solution together.

4 ***Active encouragement for each other's abilities.*** Your abilities may seem unimportant to me, and mine may seem insignificant to you. Yet those personal abilities are gifts given by our Creator to help us carve out our own unique places in the world. It is important for me to look beyond my own world of self to acknowledge a God-given gift in another.

5 Accepting fair and appropriate disagreements. In any relationship there will always be disagreements. What matters is how they are handled. Ask the question, "How important is it?" Will the outcome of the disagreement really matter, or do I just need to be right? In a relationship of unconditional love, two persons can always agree to disagree, while continuing to care for each other!

6 Respect for each other's rights. No relationship is healthy that requires one person to be subservient. Your rights are important, and so are mine. When either you or I think, "My rights are being chronically disrespected," it's time to take a hard look at the relationship and see just what is going on, and how things can change.

7 Being able to express anger safely. Many of us have been taught that expressing anger is wrong, and therefore when we feel angry, we also feel guilty for feeling it! Yet anger is one of the useful emotions we possess when we are born into the world. Properly expressed, anger is a force for healthy, positive change. There are two things we cannot do with anger, if we hope to remain emotionally healthy. One is to act out violently. The other is "stuffing" our anger inside ourselves. How much better to say, "I feel very angry right now about what's happened. I want to discuss it, but first I need to cool down. Can we meet in several hours to talk?"

8 Respect for and talking about feelings. The saying "You shouldn't feel that way!" has caused much unnecessary human suffering and guilt. "But I *do* feel that way!" I protest. We feel how we feel, and there is no denying those feelings. Our feelings may be the deepest expression of our humanity. In order to be understood by another human being and to better understand that person, we can learn to invite and encourage "feeling" language. Feelings matter!

9 Willingness to negotiate and compromise. "My way or the highway" is a poor foundation for a relationship! Two of the most important skills we can gain to see us through life are negotiation and compromise. Negotiation means, "I give up something to get something, and you give up something to get something." Compromise, handled well, means "you win, I win, we both win"!

10 Maturity and restraint in any exercise of authority. At certain times authority must be exercised — for example, when someone is behaving in compulsive ways, and the relationship partner must intervene. Screaming and yelling do not build loving relationships; they only scar the soul. "I care very deeply about you, but I can't stand by any longer and watch you do this to yourself or to our relationship" is a much kinder approach.

11 Equal treatment of each other. The Golden Rule — "Do unto others as you would have them do unto you" — is a time-tested basis for healthy relationships. When I follow it, I may occasionally be disappointed, but I don't have to stoop to treating you less fairly. If I recognize that I am being exploited or abused, then it will be wise for me to detach. But if I treat you as I want to be treated, most of the time I will receive the treatment I desire.

12 Freedom to make mistakes and to accept another's mistakes. No person is perfect. All of us make mistakes. It's just part of being human. If I can accept ahead of time the reality that I will make mistakes, I can tolerate it when it happens. And if I recognize that you will also make human mistakes, I can tolerate your mistakes as well. Every mistake contains a lesson. "Progress, not perfection," is what the "Big Book" of Alcoholics Anonymous teaches — a fine rule of life.

13 Willingness to say, "I was wrong." Those three words are so painful to say, but so healing when said. If a considerable length of time has passed before we realize our error, it's tempting to rationalize, "That was so long ago, there's no point in going back now." But admitting one's errors is basic to spiritual growth. Until it's done, that old poison festers deep down inside. The admission, once made, brings with it a grace-filled opportunity to make amends. Reaching out to another person in honesty to confess a wrong and set things right helps both souls to grow.

14 Willingness to listen to each other's fears. Sharing my fear with a trusted person invariably shrinks that fear. And as we talk about it further, the fear shrinks even more, until I see that, together, we can meet any fear with equanimity. As we become better able to face life on life's terms, we find the strength to face our fears and depend on faith to carry us through.

15 Expressing affection and warmth, without intruding. Someone has said we need eleven hugs a day just to be healthy emotionally. Yet some days I wonder if I could stand even one! My boundaries change daily, according to a great many variables in my life. Sometimes I feel open and outgoing, at other times I feel the need for "space" and solitude. In terms of physical expressions of love, every individual's choice of saying "Yes" or "No" deserves to be respected in full.

16 Respecting each other's privacy. Living together calls for delicacy by all involved. The wife of a famous Broadway composer said her recipe for a happy marriage was "Two bathrooms!" However you work it out, couples need to recognize that some places and times are inviolable. Even when great mutual honesty exists, personal privacy is vital to the good of the relationship.

17 Respect and encouragement for individual differences. Each of us is unique, original, not exactly like anyone else who has ever lived. Encouraging our partner in all those things that make him or her unique is one way we can express our appreciation for the privilege of living with a completely original human being. After all, we chose the person in the first place because he or she was different from the rest of the world! As our relationship builds, it's important to continue cherishing those differences.

18 Mutual honesty. Successful relationships have a foundation of trust, and honesty is the basic component of trust. In order to trust you, I must know that what you say is true, that you can be counted on, that you are not deceiving me in any way. And of course it works the other way as well. You need to know how I really feel, what I'm willing to do, what I need, and that what I say is the way it is. That kind of honesty is the basis for a trusting, lasting partnership.

19 Equal sharing of financial resources. In some relationships both partners bring in equal funds, while in others, one partner contributes the majority of the financial resources. Yet it is crucial for both to share in whatever belongs to the partnership. At times one person may have a specific need greater than he or she can manage alone.

If the partner supports that need, the relationship is strengthened, for one day the tables may be turned, and the one who supported can now ask for and receive support.

20 Celebrating every accomplishment, no matter how small. Some of us grew up in families where any achievement was met by a statement something like this: "You're supposed to make the honor roll. It's nothing to get puffed up about!" Many families believe that complimenting children fosters conceit, and therefore they only comment on what the children do wrong — never what they do right. It's never too late to have a happy childhood! Supporting each other with affirmation, validation, and increased respect expands and enlarges our souls.

20 Ways to Celebrate Me and Savor My Life

1 I do unto myself as I would do unto others. We may tend to focus so much on other people and their needs that we neglect ourselves. When I remember that I was created by a loving God, self-respect and self-care are the appropriate response. Being generous with myself helps me learn how to be truly generous with others.

2 I forgive my own trespasses, as I forgive those of others. A great thing about life is that it gives us an infinite number of opportunities to learn necessary lessons and life skills. When I goof up, life doesn't hold that goof against me forever. Instead, life invites me to just pick up the pieces and move ahead. And if life is that forgiving, surely I can be the same.

3 I realize I do not have to be and do everything for everyone. Sometimes we behave as if we are the rulers of all things. When we do too much for other people, we may tell ourselves we do it out of a desire to serve. Yet in reality we may be arrogantly assuming that no one else can do the thing as well as we can. When I take over, I rob the other person of the opportunity to take pride in his or her success. A reliable indicator of whether I am doing too much for others is whether I habitually step in before anyone even asks for my help.

4 I set realistic goals and am prepared to change them. Setting goals is the only way to achieve them. Yet a goal is of little use unless it is accompanied by an action plan. What step must I take, today, this week, next week, to move me closer to my goals? Action steps are specific tasks I accomplish to get me where I want to go. My goals need to be do-able, not so lofty that they overwhelm me before I even begin. If my goals are attainable, as I reach one after another of the simpler ones, my confidence grows and I can set even more ambitious goals. If I discover at some point that my goals are not rewarding ones, I am always free to exchange those goals for new ones.

5 I realize that many problems are not my fault. Growing up in a dysfunctional family, many of us came to believe that we were the cause of everything that went wrong. Even if I was responsible for a problem now and again, no one is so important as to be the cause of all life's problems! I accept responsibility for my own behavior and actions, but I no longer accept responsibility for the actions of others that are beyond my control. One way to measure how realistic my sense of responsibility is to notice how often I say, "I'm sorry." "I'm sorry" is appropriate if it means, "I am sad I did this, or sad that this has happened to you, and I want you to know it." However, if I find myself always saying "I'm sorry" as a sort of general apology for my existence on the planet, I deserve to free myself from unending self-blame.

6 I get regular and sustained exercise on a near-daily basis. Exercise is nothing more than a well-established habit. I wouldn't dream of beginning my public day without brushing my teeth. It's a habit I learned in childhood. Teaching myself to exercise regularly is much the same. If I do it regularly and faithfully for thirty days, it will become a habit I can maintain. Again, do-able goals are key. I prefer to start with a fifteen-minute walk along the sidewalks of my neighborhood, then build up to something more challenging. Strengthening and taking care of my body is one way that I express gratitude for the gift of life.

7 I get adequate rest and sleep on a regular basis. Sleep helps the human organism to repair the damage done by our daily pursuits. If I fail to give my mind and body time to restore themselves, my body and mind will suffer. Setting a regular bedtime, getting up at a regular time every day, avoiding experiences or substances that overstimulate me, and dedicating my bedroom to rest rather than entertainment help me to obtain that needed nightly renewal. If I have trouble sleeping because of a nagging worry or concern, as soon as I realize I am obsessing about my problem, I visualize myself offering up the problem to my Higher Power: "I can't handle this, so I'm turning it over to You." And then I visualize my Higher Power taking the problem from me. After that I can lie down and go back to sleep, trusting that all will be well.

8 I stay in touch with Nature and the Great Outdoors. In recent times we human beings have put up all sorts of walls between ourselves and the natural world — heavily insulated houses, double and triple panes of glass, air-conditioning and central heat that require closed windows, and over-reliance on television. A day in the woods, on a mountaintop, or at an uncrowded beach can help us to get back in touch with the wonders of Nature and the miracle of the created world. When we do that and understand ourselves as an integral part of the natural world, we can cherish the Creation and ourselves in it.

9 I take a "Me Day" once in a while. Businesses recognize sick days — why not well days? An occasional

Wellness Day away from my place of work would go far toward restoring my enthusiasm for my job and ability to work effectively. If a Wellness Day away from the job isn't possible, then I can take a special day for myself — a day when I do only those things that feed my spirit. Refreshment may come from digging in the earth, writing a poem, or giving a worn piece of furniture a fresh coat of paint. I may want to stretch out in a canoe and just drift under a summer sky, or climb into a hammock with something great to read. When I consider how many days I give to other people, I realize that I deserve a whole day of my own now and again.

10 I choose to eat health-giving foods and avoid foods that are destructive to my well-being. No matter how delicious that sugar- and fat-laden pastry may seem, or how juicy that marbled prime rib roast may appear, I know that my body will be better without them. The key is one little word: *think!* If I cultivate the habit of thinking about what I eat before I eat it, I will choose more wisely. Before I put the food in my mouth, I can *think* how I will feel after I have finished eating. Will I feel nourished, or badly fed? I will be helped in doing this by chewing slowly and savoring every mouthful before I take another bite.

11 I deal with my fears of ageing. Human beings naturally seem to resist the notion that we are all growing older day by day. Yet if we stop to consider, we begin to grow old from the moment of our birth! No one is able to halt the process, and every stage is a building-block for the one to follow. One special blessing of ageing is that older folks usually care less and less what other people think! It's okay to wish we didn't have to grow old, and good to share our feeling about it with someone who understands. It's also good to remember all those older people who were role models and wisdom guides for me. When I recognize that I can be a similar role model and wisdom guide for others, I can accept it and be glad.

12 I ask for help from friends, relatives, and professionals. "No man is an island," the poet said. People are created to be interdependent! One of life's joys is being able to help someone else, but if I don't ask for that help, I deprive someone of that satisfaction. Then, too, one person's view of any situation is always a limited one. Someone else may be able to see my situation in a different light, one that helps me to better understand. Asking for help is not an admission of weakness. It is evidence of maturity. When we admit our need and ask for help, we find that help comes from all sides and surprising sources. When you ask for my help, you are telling me, "I trust you, and I believe you have wisdom and valuable experience to share."

13 I have built structure into my life. Religious communities live by a "rule of life" — time is set aside for prayer, for worship, for recreation, and for work. One need not be a cloistered religious to have a rule of life. Fifteen minutes each morning to commune with one's Higher Power, scheduled periods of exercise, regular commitment to volunteer work, arranging special time with one's partner or one's child — these are all daily, do-able examples of building structure into one's life. Serenity comes when we order our lives to an appropriate extent, while always remaining open for the surprising, graced moment that may come at any time.

14 I don't worry about doing my work. Ideally, I choose work that is appropriate to my interests and aptitudes, work that I enjoy, work that fulfills. And then I go about doing that work to the best of my ability, without constant worry about how well I am doing. If I am unhappy in my work, that is a signal that I may want to explore other possibilities that will hold more satisfaction for me. If I choose my work well, most of the time it will not seem like work at all. I will then have the joy of knowing that I am doing what the Creator intends me to do with my life.

15 I go more than halfway to make friends. When someone moves to a new town, the Welcome Wagon often pays a call. If nothing more happens, the newcomer will still be isolated and lacking in friends. We might think of ourselves as a reverse "Welcome Wagon," seeking out groups with interests similar to our own, looking for neighbors who may be lonely too, and giving our energies to worthwhile community projects. In so doing, we will be sure to find ourselves greeting and being greeted by new friends. "Nobody ever comes to see me" is a complaint that has no merit. To have a friend, I must be a friend. It is as simple as that!

16 I don't brood if others do things I don't like. Somewhere along life's way, people will surely do things I don't like. The offenders may be people I barely know, or they may be close family and dear friends. In either case, I can nurse my grudge and become a habitually resentful person, or I can deal with it and then let it go. Sometimes it will be appropriate for me to tell the other person how I feel about what happened; at other times it's counterproductive to try. "How important is it?" is always a good question to ask. What will the result be if I continue to nurse this grudge? The result will be unhappiness on my part, while the other party goes blithely on his or her way, indifferent to my self-induced misery. Detaching is an art, and the sooner I learn it, the happier I will be.

17 I grieve my losses when they occur. Grief is a task that must be done — sooner or later. When grief is fresh, well-meaning persons around us don't always understand the importance of grieving. They may advise, "Get your mind off of it," or try to stop me from talking about my grief. When that happens, I can simply say, "It helps me to talk about this, and it will help me if you can be with me to listen." Sometimes our sadness masquerades as anger — for example, when a love affair comes to a sudden end. I may think that I am angry with the one who broke off the relationship, when in reality I am grieving because it is over. Finding someone who can just be there to listen and offer a comforting touch is the best help we can find. If we do our grieving in good time, one day the pall of sorrow will eventually lift and life will begin to hold savor for us once more.

18 I have fun whenever I can. Anyone who has survived a life-threatening illness sees every day as a precious gift to be celebrated. Those of us blessed with generally good health sometimes have to be reminded that we live in a marvelous world. If we don't feel that we're entitled, or have forgotten how to have fun, we can look back over our childhood and youth to see what was fun to us then. Yes, we grown-ups can find ways to reproduce some of those activities and feelings in our adult life. Flying a kite is great fun. So is blowing soap bubbles, or building a castle in the sand. All of those activities are fine ways to begin re-educating ourselves to have fun.

19 I expect to be stressed and even depressed at times. Is life supposed to be a tranquil, boringly mirror-like stream? I think not. Stress can sometimes be called by another name — creative tension. Human beings have risen to some of our most noble behavior under the severest stress.

This is not to say that we should seek out stress. But we need not try to insulate ourselves, unwilling to face the great adventures of life. As for depression, it can sometimes be a true illness. If you or someone you care about suffers depressive symptoms for more than a few weeks, it's wise to seek professional help. In some situations it's appropriate to be depressed — bereavement, loss of a job, failure of a cherished plan. This situational depression usually lifts once the depressed person becomes able to draw afresh from his or her own inner and outer resources. It's the combination of the light and the dark in life that makes the human struggle so richly complex.

20 Most importantly, I just keep on breathing! If we stop to think about it, the mere act of breathing is a miracle in itself. The elements available to us when we breathe may have come from far distant galaxies and universes — we might be breathing stardust! Every breath we take brings new energy, the vital oxygen that feeds our bodies, while the air we breathe out carries poisons away from our bloodstream and our lungs. What a miraculous system! Keeping on breathing, gratefully, may be the best expression we can make of our oneness with everything in this Universe.

20 Attitudes That Help Me Cope

1 There is nothing I need to do "first" in order to be a complete person. I do not have to wait until I am smart enough, educated enough, thin enough, or rich enough to have a satisfying life. I can meet life one second at a time, one minute at a time, one hour at a time, and one day at a time, making the most of the gifts of each moment. The truth is that I will never be a "complete" person, if by that I mean a "perfect" person. I have everything I need right now, today, to live fully into my life.

2 I don't have to prove myself again and again. I may have grown up hearing that other people's opinions were all-important. Today I can change that "tape." All I need is my own inner assurance that I am capable, talented, and a worthwhile person. I am continually discovering the things I do best and enjoy most, using my talents and aptitudes not to gain approval from others, but for the pleasure I find in them. As an incidental by-product, other people will naturally recognize my fulfillment as I grow in self-confidence and express my best self.

3 Learning from my past will empower me to live my life better today. There are two ways to draw on the events of the past. One is to go over them again and again, mentally beating up on myself because of how I responded. The positive way to build on the past is to ask, "What could I do better today if the same situation presented itself?" Maybe I was too trusting, or not trusting enough. Maybe my boundaries were too permeable, and I was exploited and abused. Maybe I missed out on a profitable opportunity because my caution was extreme. One good way to build on the experiences of my past is to talk them over with someone I trust, whose wisdom about life is clear. Perhaps then I will learn things about myself that can help me when the next challenge comes.

*4 **Letting go of my pessimistic thoughts will energize me.*** The world is divided into groups: those who see a glass half full, the others who see it half empty. Folks who see the glass half full see potential benefit in new situations. They believe the best about new people they meet. They give credit where credit is due and live in expectation of good things. We can teach ourselves to set aside pessimistic thinking to become positive, hopeful folks. If close friends and family tease me about my pessimistic attitudes, maybe the next time instead of getting defensive I will listen to what they are saying, laugh at my own gloom, and think of another way of looking at life. One morning my own glass will suddenly be half full!

*5 **Giving someone the benefit of the doubt will strengthen us both.*** I would rather trust and occasionally be disappointed than grow into a chronic attitude of mistrust. Giving another person the benefit of the doubt automatically frees that other person to offer his or her best. Giving the benefit of the doubt frees me to do my own thing and frees the other person to act naturally without fear of displeasing or making mistakes. It's a win/win situation for us both.

*6 **When I say no, I must mean no.*** A dependable person always matches actions to words. When I say "Yes, I will do a certain thing," I want others to be able to expect that I will do as I have promised. If I say "No," my "No" is meaningless if I cave in and do the opposite thing. Being consistent is particularly important in parenting. A parent who says "No" and then backs down and says "Yes" loses a youngster's respect. The same thing happens between adults. No matter how hard it is for me to hold the line, if "No" was my answer, I will make it stick. And every time I succeed in making my "No" effective, I will find it easier to repeat this behavior in the future.

7 I can unselfishly offer another person some of my energy. Energy is contagious! We catch it from other people when it is given with a free heart and spirit. One autumn day after I had sent my daughter out to rake up the leaves, I noticed her looking despondent and grim. I picked up the second rake, followed her out to the lawn, and simply began raking too. "What are you doing?" she asked in surprise. "I thought I would give you a hand." I said. Immediately the situation changed. Both our hearts lightened, and we found pleasure in finishing the task together. How good it is to know that we can share our energies with others when they need that lift. And our own spirits will be lifted as a result.

8 When I have wronged someone, I ask that person to forgive me. An essential part of any spiritual program is admitting wrongs and making amends. The best way is to go directly to the one we have wronged, offer our apology, ask forgiveness, and set about changing our behavior toward that person in the future. Sometimes it is not possible to approach such a person directly. The person might have died, or moved to another part of the country. Or it might be someone who became so angry that he or she will have nothing more to do with me. Approaching a person from my past may even cause difficulties for that person in his or her present situation. In such cases, a letter may be the best way of asking for forgiveness. A letter can be written to someone who has died, even read at the graveside. A letter can be written that is never mailed. The important point is that the writer of the letter accepts responsibility for the deed and makes a heartfelt decision to behave differently thereafter. That is the way of making true amends.

9 I will say only that which I mean. People often utter meaningless social pleasantries, in hopes of ingratiating themselves with the other person. Most of us have done this at one time or another, hardly thinking about what we are saying. Yet this habit of saying seemingly pleasant things without intending to follow through is a subtle character-destroyer. It diminishes other people's respect for me, and it fosters a mental habit of untruthfulness. At other times, words may be spoken in the heat of anger that we don't really mean. When I feel an explosive verbal attack on another person coming on, I will be well advised to take at least five deep breaths before speaking, and then — not speak! Taking the deep breaths gives me time to think about whether the remark, if made, would help or harm the situation. No matter how much satisfaction I might get from bursting out with hurtful words, in the long run it's best for everyone if such words are never said.

10 I will practice sharing my dreams with another. The things we dream of and believe in have the best chance of coming true. A private dream is good, but a dream shared is better, because in sharing my dream with another person, I invite that person to do whatever he or she can to help me realize my dream. Dreaming alone, I may think my dream will never be realized, but sharing it with another may help me to see what has to be done to bring it to life.

11 I can stretch myself, either by finishing one thing, or by beginning something new. Old-fashioned pride comes to the fore when a task is finished up properly. It could be that home-repair project that's been hanging fire for weeks, starting that book I promised myself to write one day, or just getting on board with the exercise program I know is long overdue. It is easy for us to get too comfortable with the status quo! We grow when we reach out, stretch ourselves, try something new, take a considered risk. Maybe it's something I had never imagined I would be able to do, such as signing up for a painting class, or learning to ski. Maybe it's making amends I've needed to make for a long time. Whatever it is, I will grow spiritually once I finish something that needs to be finished or start something that needs to be begun.

12 I can design a simple task for myself and work toward completing it. Simple — that's the magic word! I don't have to set out to run a marathon, or lose 30 pounds, or even check out that new computer program. I can walk around the block for a start! I can lose just one pound by the end of next week. I can go to the computer store and sign up for a free tutorial. And once the simplest step is accomplished, then I can take a second, and a third. Yard by yard, life is hard. Inch by inch, it's a cinch!

13 I can express my unconditional appreciation to someone. Has someone ever told you, "I like you just for yourself?" If you were fortunate enough to have such a compliment, you probably felt warm all over. It's great to know that I can give someone else that feeling of warmth and appreciation. A competent but grumpy co-worker may be amazed to hear, "You know, you did that job really well." Or a child who hears a lot of negative criticism will love "I feel really proud to have you for my daughter/son." When I tell someone of my unconditional appreciation, I do it without expecting anything in return. It's a gift freely given — one of those random acts of kindness we read about on bumper stickers — that helps both of us to bloom.

14 My maturity helps me to endure the uncertainties of life. As children, we get the idea that if we are "good" and do as we are told, everything in life will turn out just fine. Yet at some point we discover that no matter how faithfully we play by the rules, life has a knack of presenting us with experiences we would rather not have had. After a few such shocks, I could fall into the habit of living paralyzed by fear. Yet as I look back at how I have responded to the events of my life, I see that I am a strong and competent person. When I remember that my Higher Power has great plans for me, I make my way through times of uncertainty without being thrown for a loop. Nothing stays the same forever. Eventually this uncertainty will pass and I will have new guidance about what direction to take. My prayer is that rather than fearing the future, I may always keep myself receptive for the many good things that lie ahead.

15 I can teach someone a thing or two about myself. Most of us probably believe that our family and friends know all about us. Yet when I stop and ask myself how much I really know about those close to me, I realize there is much I do not know. It's good to seek out opportunities to share our life experiences, what those experiences have taught us, and our hopes and dreams. Telling our life stories is one of the most wonderful ways we have of binding our lives together. When I share about myself, you gain the courage to share something of yourself, and the result is increased understanding between us. That's *good!*

16 I can convert one of my past mistakes into a teachable moment. Every life experience has either a satisfying outcome or a disappointing one. The satisfying outcomes are great, the disappointing ones even better, because every single one includes a lesson. Even the person who pushes my buttons the most fiercely has a lesson for me. When I take the time to consider what it is about that person that gets me riled up, I may discover a manifestation of some personality trait in myself that I very much dislike — a trait I don't even like to acknowledge I have. When the woman who takes over the entire conversation or the man who tries to be the center of attention irritates me, I can probably admit that I also do things to make myself the center of attention at times. Uncomfortable feelings and experiences are some of the strongest teachers. I welcome the opportunity to grow!

17 I must first seek peace in my own backyard. Many of us fall into the habit of criticizing others, giving too many orders, and failing to take criticism or follow directions given by someone else. Some households echo all day and all night with shouting, yelling, and unpleasant words. I will do well to examine my own conduct in the everyday affairs of my home and my work. Do I give others credit, refuse to blame, seek to praise, and live an attitude of gratitude? Those are the building blocks of a rich and rewarding life. Sometimes the best thing I can do is simply to listen attentively to what others have to say and resist the temptation to react with an immediate expression of my own. Those moments of stillness and peace are often the places from which creative solutions arise. A peaceful spirit is contagious. Can I pass mine around today?

18 I can forgive someone. Carrying around resentments and grudges is a miserable way to live. Such an attitude carries with it spiritual, mental, emotional, and even physical punishments for me. Bitterness is truly a toxin to the soul, and the sooner I can let go of any bitterness in my own heart, the more serene and fulfilled I will be. If there has been a conflicted situation, I can first examine it carefully to see what my own part was in the conflict. Then, if I can find nothing that I did to create the hurt, I can pray to let go of my own pain over it. Forgiveness doesn't come overnight, and it is never accompanied by true forgetfulness. But if I can forgive myself for my errors and pray to forgive the other person, eventually that inner release will come. I will be the better for it regardless of whether the other person is ready to forgive me. In this complex and sometimes chaotic world, a heart at peace is a treasure to be cultivated.

19 I can't be reconciled to another before I find it within myself. All of us have known moments where it was truly delicious to feel sorry for ourselves, to think harsh thoughts about another, even to wish another person ill if that person has mistreated us. And so, before I can be reconciled with someone, I have to come to the point of wanting that reconciliation. The best thing for me to do is to pray to want it. I may even have to pray that I will be able to pray to want it! Healing of any situation after deep hurt is a slow process. The healing will proceed more quickly if both persons want the reconciliation and take steps toward it. Yet even when I am the only one wanting it, I can make peace with that other person in my heart. Confessing my feelings to someone I trust is a good way to begin. Asking prayerfully to be led through the process is another fine step to take. Somewhere along the way I may have to do some forgiving of myself. When I have done that, I will be able to draw closer to the other.

20 Life will continue on with me or around me. It's my choice. There are two kinds of people in the world — the ones pitching, batting, and running the bases, and those sitting in the bleachers. Given a choice, I will become a player. If I'm giving life my best effort, using my aptitudes and skills, seeking peace and harmony with those around me while always moving toward a higher goal, I am doing something worthwhile and even noble. I will surely find greater pleasure in the activities of my day than those who are merely spectators of the game of life. I know that my efforts will influence the way my life game goes, and I will take pride in what I can achieve.

ADDITIONAL RESOURCES

Workshops and Seminars facilitated by Joseph C. Buccilli, Ph.D.

Some of the topics Dr. Buccilli has offered include the following:

- ✦ Learning to Let Go of the Past
- ✦ Getting Over Overreacting to Others
- ✦ When You're Too Busy to Get Close to Your Children
- ✦ Help For Caretakers of Ageing Parents
- ✦ How to Stop Being Victimized by Your Anxieties
- ✦ Thawing Out Frozen Feelings
- ✦ Secrets of Coping With Difficult People
- ✦ What To Do When You've Lost That Loving Feeling
- ✦ How to Cope When You've Lost Your Job
- ✦ Growing Beyond the Pain of: Having an Alcoholic Dad; Having an Alcoholic Mom
- ✦ Growing Beyond the Damage Done by: A Mother Who Hated Men; A Father Who Hated Women
- ✦ Navigating the Blended Family Maze
- ✦ Coping With the Breakdown of a Relationship
- ✦ Coming to Terms With Your Feelings of Shame
- ✦ What to Do When You're Angry at God
- ✦ How to Cope in the Absence of Strong Family Support
- ✦ Help for Those Who Feel They Were Parental Failures
- ✦ How to Cope When Your Child is Lesbian/Gay
- ✦ Healing the Emotional Wounds of Miscarriage or Abortion
- ✦ Help for Parents With a Chemically Dependent Child
- ✦ Coping When Your Child Has Been Abused or Raped
- ✦ Coping With Your Inability to Conceive or Bear a Child

Other mutually agreed-upon topics can be chosen.

For more information, call

(609) 629-4441

or write

Joseph C. Buccilli, Ph.D.
P.O. Box 709
Sicklerville, New Jersey 08081

More Books from Recovery Communications, Inc.

available through your local bookstore

Toby Rice Drews. **Getting Them Sober, Volume One — You Can Help!** Hundreds of ideas for sobriety & recovery. The million-seller endorsed by Dr. Norman Vincent Peale and "Dear Abby."

Toby Rice Drews. **Getting Them Sober, Volume Four — Separations & Healings.** All about detachment and separation issues for alcoholic families.

Jennifer J. Richardson, M.S.W. **Diary of Abuse/Diary of Healing.** A young girl's secret journal recording two decades of family abuse, with an inspirational message of hope for other abuse survivors.

Betsy Tice White. **Mountain Folk, Mountain Food: Down-Home Wisdom, Plain Tales, and Recipe Secrets from Appalachia.** The joy of living as expressed in charming vignettes and mouth-watering regional foods!

Betsy Tice White. **Turning Your Teen Around: How A Couple Helped Their Troubled Son While Keeping Their Marriage Alive and Well.** One family's successful personal battle against teen-age drug use, with dozens of powerfully helpful tips for parents in pain.

And coming soon:

Linda Meyer, Ph.D. **I See Myself Changing: A Meditation Journal.** For the young and the young at heart.

The Getting Them Sober Foundation℠

founded by **Toby Rice Drews,**
author of the world-renowned
Getting Them Sober book series

is created to help families recover from the craziness of living with alcoholism.

Call or write today to find out how you can help!

The Getting Them Sober Foundation℠
P.O. Box 50128
Baltimore, Maryland 21211
Phone:
(410) 243-8352